William Lowes Rushton

Shakespeare's Testamentary Language

//

William Lowes Rushton

Shakespeare's Testamentary Language

ISBN/EAN: 9783337055233

Printed in Europe, USA, Canada, Australia, Japan

Cover: Foto ©Thomas Meinert / pixelio.de

More available books at **www.hansebooks.com**

SHAKESPEARE'S

TESTAMENTARY LANGUAGE

BY

WILLIAM LOWES RUSHTON

OF GRAY'S INN, BARRISTER-AT-LAW

Corresponding Member of the Berlin Society for the Study of Modern
Languages ; Author of 'Shakespeare a Lawyer,' 'Shakespeare's Legal
Maxims,' 'Shakespeare Illustrated by the Lex Scripta,'
'Shakespeare Illustrated by Old Authors,' &c.

LONDON
LONGMANS, GREEN, AND CO.
1869

NOTICE.

———◆———

MANY of these illustrations were laid before the Berlin Society for the Study of Modern Languages on the 4th day of February, 1861, and were published in the Archiv für das Studium der neueren Sprachen und Literaturen, XXXI. Band. Shakespeare Illustrated by the Lex Scripta has appeared in the Archiv f. n. Sprachen, but has not yet been published in England.

4 ULLET LANE, AIGBURTH ROAD,
LIVERPOOL:
Long Vacation, 1868.

SHAKESPEARE'S

TESTAMENTARY LANGUAGE.

—◆—

IN the commencement of the old forms of wills, the testator generally mentions the sickness of his body, and the soundness of his mind or memory.

Madfolkes and Lunatic persons, during the time of their furor or insanitie of minde, cannot make a testament, nor dispose anie thing by will, no not *ad pias causas*: The reason is most forcible, because they knowe not what they do; for in making of testaments the integrity or perfitnes of minde and not health of the body is requisite; and there upon arose that common clause, used in every testament almost, *sick in body, but of perfit minde and memory.**

Ben.   Tell me in sadness, who is that you love.
Rom.   What, shall I groan and tell thee ?

* *A Briefe Treatise of Testaments and Last Willes.* By Henrie Swinburn, Bachelar of Civill Lawe.   London: printed by John Windet, 1590.   The Second Part, page 37.

B

Ben.   Groan! why, no;
But sadly tell me who.

Rom.   Bid a *sick man* in sadness *make his will*:
Ah, word ill urged to one that is so ill!
In sadness, cousin, I do love a woman.

Romeo and Juliet, Act i. Sc. 1.

Anne.   Now, Master Slender,—
Slen.   Now, good Mistress Anne,—
Anne.   What is your will?
Slen.   My will! 'od's heartlings, that's a pretty jest
indeed!   I ne'er made my will yet, I thank heaven; I
am not such a *sickly creature*, I give heaven praise.

Merry Wives of Windsor, Act iii. Sc. 4.

Pain.   Good as the best.   Promising is the very air
o' the time: it opens the eyes of expectation: performance is ever the duller for his act; and, but in the plainer
and simpler kind of people, the deed of saying is quite
out of use.   To promise is most courtly and fashionable:
performance is a kind of *will or testament* which argues
a great *sickness* in his judgement that makes it.

Timon of Athens, Act v. Sc. 1.

To this practice or usual clause in old wills
Romeo, Slender, and the Painter partly allude,
that is, to the statement of sickness.

I, Nicholas Gybson, citizen and grocer of London,
whole of mind and of perfect remembrance, albeit *sick of
body*, make this my present Will and Testament, as well
concerning the order and disposition of my goods,
chattels, and other things moveable, as of my lands and
tenements, rents, reversions, and services, and hereditaments whatsoever.—*Co. Rep.*

I, Chr. Digges, of St. Gregory's without the walls of the City of Canterbury, Esqr., son and heir of Will. Digges, late of Barham in the County of Kent, deceased, being *sick in body*, but of good and perfect remembrance, thanked be Almighty God, revoking and making void all and other my former Wills, ordain and make this my present Testament and last Will.—*Co. Rep.*

Sometimes in the beginning the testator commends or bequeathes his soul to God or his Creator, and his body to the earth. To this practice these passages refer:—

This brief abridgement of my will I make :
My soul and body to the skies and ground;
My resolution, husband, do thou take ;
Mine honour be the knife's that makes my wound;
My shame be his that did my fame confound ;
   And all my fame that lives disbursed be
   To those that live, and think no shame of me.
Lucrece.

Carlisle.   Many a time hath banish'd Norfolk fought
For Jesu Christ in glorious Christian field,
Streaming the ensign of the Christian cross
Against black pagans, Turks, and Saracens ;
And toil'd with works of war, retired himself
To Italy ; and there at Venice gave
His body to that pleasant country's earth,
And his pure soul unto his captain Christ,
Under whose colours he had fought so long.
Richard II., Act iv. Sc. 1.

Aum.   Where is the duke my father with his power ?

K. Rich. No matter where; of comfort no man
  speak :
Let's talk of graves, of worms and epitaphs ;
Make dust our paper and with rainy eyes
Write sorrow on the bosom of the earth,
Let's choose executors and talk of wills :
And yet not so, for what can we *bequeath*
Save our deposed bodies to the ground ?
Our lands, our lives and all are Bolingbroke's,
And nothing can we call our own but death
And that small model of the barren earth
Which serves as paste and cover to our bones.
Richard II., Act iii. Sc. 2.

First, I give and *bequeath my soul unto Almighty God*
my Maker, Redeemer, and Saviour, and *my body to be
buried* where it shall please God, after the discretion of
my beloved wife, Alice Gybson, my sole executrix under
written.—*Co. Rep.* The Will of Nicholas Gybson.

And Shakespeare's will commences in this
manner :—

In the name of God, amen ! I, William Shackspeare,
of Stratford-upon-Avon in the Countie of Warr., gent.,
in perfect health and memorie, God be praysed, doe
make and ordayne this my last will and testament in
manner and forme followeing, that ys to saye, ffirst, I
comend *my soule into the handes of God my Creator*, hop-
ing and assuredlie beleeving, through thonelie merits of
Jesus Christe my Saviour, to be made partaker of lyfe
everlastinge, and my *bodye to the earth* whereof yt ys
made.

Pericles. I'll make my will then, and, as *sick men* do
Who know the world, see heaven, but, feeling woe,

Gripe not at earthly joys as erst they did ;
So I *bequeath* a happy peace to you
And all good men, as every prince should do ;
My riches to the earth from whence they came ;
But my unspotted fire of love to you.

Act i. Sc. 1.

Pericles alludes to this testamentary statement of sickness, and he makes a sort of
parody on the bequest of soul and body; in
other words, instead of bequeathing his soul.
he bequeathes a happy peace and his unspotted fire of love, and instead of bequeathing his body he bequeathes his riches to the
earth from whence they came: and Arthur, in
King John, Act iv., Sc. 3—

> *Arthur.*   O me! my uncle's spirit is in these stones :
> Heaven take my soul, and England keep my bones.
> *King John*, Act iv. Sc. 3.

—seems to refer to the bequest of soul and
body.

> *Diana.*   O, behold this ring,
> Whose high respect and rich validity
> Did lack a parallel; yet for all that
> He gave it to a commoner o' the camp,
> If I be one.
> *Count.*   He blushes, and 'tis it :
> Of six preceding ancestors, that *gem*,
> Conferr'd by testament to the sequent issue,

Hath it been owed and worn.   This is his wife;
That ring's a thousand proofs.
> *All's Well that Ends Well*, Act v. Sc. 3.

                            Give me that *ring*.
Ber.   I'll lend it thee, my dear; but have no power
To give it from me.
    Dia.   Will you not, my lord?
    Ber.   It is an honour 'longing to our house,
Bequeathed down from many ancestors;
Which were the greatest obloquy i' the world
In me to lose.
    Dia.   Mine honour's such a *ring*:
My chastity's the jewel of our house,
Bequeathed down from many ancestors;
Which were the greatest obloquy i' the world
In me to lose.
> *All's Well that Ends Well*, Act iv. Sc. 2.

The gem or ring said in these passages to
have been conferred by testament to the
sequent issue, and bequeathed down from
many ancestors, seems to answer, in some
respects at least, the descriptions given in
our old law books of an heirloom, which, says
Coke, is ' a word comprehending divers implements of household stuff or furniture, as a
marble hearth, the first best bed, and other
things which, by the custom of some places,
have belonged to a house for certain *descents*,
and are such as are never inventoried after the

death of the owner as chattels, and therefore never go to the executor or administrator, but to the heir along with the house itself by custom, and not by the common law. For a man by the common law cannot be heir to goods and chattels.'—(I. Inst. 18 b.; 185 b.)

Heir-loom (says Cowell) seemeth to be compounded of heir and loom, that is, a frame to weave in; the word by time hath a more general signification than at first it did bear, comprehending all implements of household, as tables, presses, cupboards, bedsteads, wainscot, and such like; which, by the custom of some counties, having belonged to a *house* certain *descents,* are never *inventoried* after the decease of the owner as chattels, but accrue to the heir with the house by custom.

Helena. A ring the county wears,
That downward hath succeeded in his house
From son to son, some four or five *descents*
Since the first father wore it : this ring he holds
In most rich choice ; yet in his idle fire,
To buy his will, it would not seem too dear,
Howe'er repented after.
All's Well, Act iii. Sc. 7.

The reader will perceive that Coke and Cowell, in their description of heir-looms, speak of things which, by the custom of some places and counties, had belonged to a house certain *descents,* and that Helena speaks of a ring the county wears,

That downward hath succeeded in his house
From son to son, some four or five *descents*.

The ancient jewels of the crown are heir-looms, and shall descend to the next successor, and are not devisable by testament. For the law preferreth the custom before the devise.—*Wood's Inst.*, 2nd ed., pp. 66, 67.

Consuetudo Hundredi de Stretford in Com. Oxon. est quod haeredes tenementorum infra hundredum praedictum existentium post mortem antecessorum suorum habebunt, &c., principalium, Anglicè, an heir-loom, viz. de quodam genere catallorum, utensilium, &c. optimum plaustrum, optimam carucam, optimum, &c.—*Co. Litt.*, 18 b.

According to some authorities heir-looms consist only of articles of a large size, as benches, tables, cupboards fixed to the freehold. For example, Spelman, in describing an heir-loom, says, ' omne utensile robustius quod ab aedibus non facilè revellitur, ideoque ex more quorundam locorum ad haeredem transit, tanquam membrum haereditas.' (Gloss., voce Heir-loom.) But such bulky articles would be more properly described as fixtures.

Vio. 'Tis beauty truly blent, whose red and white
Nature's own sweet and cunning hand laid on :
Lady, you are the cruell'st she alive,
If you will lead these graces to the grave
And leave the world no copy.
  Oli. O, sir, I will not be so hard-hearted ; I will give out divers *schedules* of my beauty : it shall be *inventoried*,

and every particle and utensil *labelled* to my will: as, item, two lips, indifferent red; item, two grey eyes, with lids to them; item, one neck, one chin, and so forth. Were you sent here to *praise* me? *

Twelfth Night, Act i. Sc. 5.

Inventory, inventorium, is a list, a *schedule* containing a full and true description of all the goods and chattels of a testator at the time of his death, with their value appraised by indifferent persons, which every executor or administrator ought to exhibit to the Bishop or ordinary at such time as he shall appoint. (West. Symb., part I., lib. 2, sec. 396.)

The word label has two significations: it signifies a paper annexed by way of addition or explication to a will or testament, which is called a codicil or label (Cowell, Interpr.), and in this sense it may be used by Olivia, who says, ' I will give out divers schedules of my beauty: it shall be inventoried, and every particle and utensil *labelled* to my will.' The word label also signifies a slip of paper or parchment for an appending seal ; and to understand thoroughly the following passage in Richard II., the idea of such a label is necessary.

* Praise, see p. 38.

B 3

York. What seal is that, that hangs without thy
    bosom ?
Yea, look'st thou pale ? let me see the writing.
    Aum. My lord, 'tis nothing.
    York.   No matter, then, who see it :
I will be satisfied ; let me see the writing.
    Aum. I do beseech your grace to pardon me :
It is a matter of small consequence,
Which for some reasons I would not have seen.
    York. Which for some reasons, sir, I mean to see.
I fear, I fear,—
    Duch.   What should you fear ?
'Tis nothing but some bond, that he is enter'd into
For gay apparel 'gainst the triumph day.
    York. Bound to himself ! what doth he with a bond
That he is bound to ? Wife, thou art a fool.
Boy, let me see the writing.

Act v. Sc. 2.

The seal York noticed hanging without
Aumerle's bosom was appended to such a
label or slip of parchment; and in this sense
the word is also used by Juliet—

> God join'd my heart and Romeo's, thou our hands ;
> And ere this hand, by thee to Romeo seal'd,
> Shall be the label to another deed,
> Or my true heart with treacherous revolt
> Turn to another, this shall slay them both.
>
> *Romeo and Juliet*, Act iii. Sc. 1.

who implies that Romeo was a deed to which
her hand had been attached as a label, and she

states what she would do ere that hand should
be a label to another deed, in other words, ere
she would marry Paris or any other man.

Antony. But here's a parchment with the seal of
    Cæsar:
I found it in his closet, 'tis his *will.*
Let but the commons hear this *testament.*

Julius Cæsar, Act iii. Sc. 2.

It may seeme that a testament and a last will be both
one thing, and that there is no difference betwixt the
one and the other, at least heere in England, because
we have no necessarie use of those solemn testaments,
in making whereof, the presence of vii. witnesses, together with observation of many moe ceremonies, is necessarily requisite by the Civill lawe. On the contrary,
it seemeth that they are not both one; partly because
they have diverse names, which doth import diversitie
of things; especially because they have different definitions: for it is received for an infallible axiome, that the
definitions being different, the things defined are diverse.
As for the former reason, it may be thus answered.
That albeit our Testaments be unsolemne, yet it doth
not follow that therefore we have no testaments, or that
our testaments are therefore meere last willes. For an
unsolemne testament is a testament, and that properlie
or in strict interpretation, as hereafter shall be confirmed,
when wee shall speake of unsolemne testaments. And
so the conclusion seemeth rather necessary then pro-
bable, that a testament and a last will are not both one,
but different. Notwithstanding, this conclusion is not
simply or perpetually true, for in some respects they are
both one, though in other respects they differ. Under-

stand, therefore, that a testament may be taken two manner of wayes: largely, and strictly. It is said to be taken largely or generally when the signification of the bare name or word Testament (which in Latin is Testamentum) is had in consideration. This word Testamentum is as much as Testatio mentis, that is to say, a testifying or witnessing of the minde. So writeth the worthy Emperour Justinian, after Sulpitius, which deduction others (without cause, I confesse, yet not without scofs) doe sharply reprehend. As though, forsooth, Justinian or Sulpitius had contended to deliver the very Etymologie of the worde Testament, and not a certaine Allusion rather of the voice onely. When this word testament is uttered in this generall sence, it differeth not from a last will; and any last will, be it a Codicill or other kinde, may be so tearmed a Testament, that is to say, a testifying, or declaring of the minde. And hence it is that not only in our speech, but in our writinges also, *wee use the tearmes of Testament and Last Will indifferently, or one for another.* It is taken strictly, when it is accepted according to that definition invented by Ulpianus, hereafter ensuing, and being taken in that sence, it differeth from a last will, yet not as opposite thereunto, but as the speciall differeth from the generall, for every Testament is a Last Will, but every Last Will is not a Testament. To speake more plainly, thus they differ: a Last Will is a generall word, and agreeth to every several kind of last will or testament: But a testament properly understoode, is one kinde of last will, even that wherein *Executor* is named. For by the naming of an Executor it differeth from the rest.—*Swinburn,* 3.

All. The will! the testament!
Sec. Cit. They were villains, murderers: the will! read the will.

Ant. You will compel me, then, to read the will?
Then make a ring about the corpse of Cæsar,
And let me show you him that made the will.
Julius Cæsar, Act iii. Sc. 2.

King Richard. Let's choose *executors* and talk of *wills*:
And yet not so, for what can we *bequeath*
Save our deposed bodies to the ground?
Our *lands*, our lives and all are Bolingbroke's,
And nothing can we call our own but death
And that small model of the barren earth
Which serves as paste and cover to our bones.
Richard II., Act iii. Sc. 2.

So Shakespeare, as in these passages, makes
no distinction between the terms Testament
and Last Will, but uses them indifferently, or
one for another.

Fourth Cit. We'll hear the will: read it, Mark
Antony.
All. The will, the will! we will hear Cæsar's will.
Ant. Have patience, gentle friends, I must not read it;
It is not meet you know how Cæsar loved you.
You are not wood, you are not stones, but men;
And, being men, hearing the *will* of Cæsar,
It will inflame you, it will make you mad:
'Tis good you know not that you are his *heirs*;
For, if you should, O, what would come of it!
Julius Cæsar, Act iii. Sc. 2.

Our Common Law calls him heir who succeeds by
right of blood to any man's lands or tenements in fee,
for by the Common Law nothing passeth jure hereditatis
but only the fee; moveables or chattels immoveable are

given by testament to whom the testator listeth, or else are at the disposition of the ordinary, to be distributed as he in conscience thinketh meet.—*Cowell.*

But Shakespeare in this passage evidently makes Antony use the word heir in the sense in which it is used by the civilians, who call heredem, qui ex testamento succedit in universum jus testatoris.

———

Since the publication of my first attempt to illustrate obscure passages in the works of Shakespeare,* it has been suggested that Shakespeare may have drawn his own Will, and that in disposing of his second best bed with the furniture in these words, 'Item I gyve unto my wief my second best bed with the furniture,' he shows his technical skill, by omitting the word devise, which he had used in disposing of the realty.† This statement has been made in ignorance of the ancient legal signification of the word devise; for although the word devise is now applied by Real Property Lawyers to real property, and

* *Shakespeare a Lawyer.* (See Appendix A.)

† Lord Campbell: *Shakespeare's Legal Acquirements Considered,* p. 105. (See Appendix B.)

the word bequeath to personal property, yet
such distinction was not made in Shakespeare's
time. The word devise is used in the disposition of the real estate in Shakespeare's Will,
together with the word bequeath, which is not
now applied to real estate ; moreover, the
word devise, in connection with the word
bequeath, is applied in another part of Shakespeare's Will to personal property, namely, to
the sum of one hundred and fifty pounds.

If the *devise* be of goods ; as when the testator dooth
bequeath his signet, his books, or his horse, &c., first to
one person, and afterwards to another person : then in
case the second legacie be simple (I meane without mention of the former), the former legacie is not taken away,
but the two legataries concurring, ought to divide the
legacie betwixt them.—*Swinburn*, 284.

A legacie (otherwise tearmed of our common lawyers
a Devise) is a gift lefte by the deceased, to bee paide
or performed by the executor, or administrator.—*Swinburn*, 15.

Suppose that in the testament it is written, that the
testator dooth *bequeath* such *landes* to such person to have
and to holde to him and to his assignes for evermore.
Howsoever in this *devise* there is not any mention of
heires, without which worde an estate of inheritance cannot passe, by any deed or gift made whiles a man yet
liveth ; yet because in testaments, the wil and the in-
tent of the testator is preferred before formal or prescript

wordes, an estate of inheritance dooth thereby passe, as if he had made expresse mention of his heires.—*Swinburn*, 191.

The *goodes* of the church can not be *devised* by testament. But the corne growing upon the glebe, and certaine other *goods*, may be *bequeathed*. Those thinges which after the death of the testator, descende to the heire of the deceased, and not to his executor, can not bee devised by testament, except in such cases where it is lawfull to devise landes, tenementes, or hereditaments. And therefore if a man seased of landes in fee or fee taile, *bequeath his trees* growing upon the said land at the time of his death, this *devise* is not good except as before.—*Swinburn*, 93.

Concerning the second kind of thinges deviseable by testament, namelie goods and chattelles; this may be delivered for a rule: That all manner of goods and chattelles maie be *bequeathed* or *devised* by will or testament, certaine cases onelie excepted. Which rule is cleane contrarie to the former of the devise of lands, tenements and hereditaments; for they can not be *devised*, saving where some custome or statute hath gained libertie, of *bequeathing or devising* of the same.—*Swinburn*, 91.

Divisa: A last will or devise of worldly goods.— (Cowell.) Notum facio quod apud Waltham feci *divisam* meam de quadam parte *pecuniae* meae in hunc modum Testamen. Hen. II. apud Gervas Dorobern. sub ann. 1182.

The word devise cometh of the French Divisir, separare, or deviser to confer unto, and is properly attributed in our Common Law to him that bequeaths his goods, by his last will and testament in writing: and the reason

is, because those that now appertain only to the devisor,
by this act are *distributed* into many parts.—*Cowell.*

XIII.

Therein three sisters dwelt of sundry sort,
The children of one syre by mothers three;
Who, *dying* whylome, did *divide* this fort
To them by equall shares in equall fee.
Spenser's *Faerie Queene*, Book ii. Canto 2.

And I think Shakespeare understood the pre-
cise legal signification of this term, for he
makes Falstaff say in the ‘Merry Wives of
Windsor,’ Act v. Sc. 5—

Divide me like a bribe buck, each a haunch : I will
keep my sides to myself, my shoulders for the fellow of
this walk, and my horns I *bequeath* your husbands. Am
I a woodman, ha ? Speak I like Herne the hunter ?
Why, now is Cupid a child of conscience : he makes
restitution. As I am a true spirit, welcome !

Shakespeare may, in this passage, play
upon the word woodman, using it in the sense
of a forester or huntsman, in connection with
Herne the hunter, and in the sense of a
mad or *wood* man in connection with the
words divide and bequeath, because, as Swinburn says, in his Briefe Treatise of Testa- ·
ments and Last Willes, ‘Madfolkes and luna-
ticke persons, during the furor or insanitie of
minde, cannot make a testament, nor dispose

of any thing by will;' and Falstaff having used the words divide and bequeath, may imply, in asking whether he is a woodman, that he has that 'integritie or perfitnesse of mind' which is requisite in making.testaments.

Item omnes viduae de cetero possint *legare* blada sua de terra sua, tam de dotibus suis, quam de aliis terris, et tenementis suis; salvis consuetudinibus, et servitiis dominorum de feodo, quæ de dotibus, et aliis tenementis suis debentur. Also from henceforth widows may bequeath the crop of their ground, as well of their dowers, as of other lands and tenements, saving to the lords of the fee, all such services as be due for their dowers and other tenements. This, the second chapter of the Statute of Merton and the translation as they appear in Coke's 2 Inst. 80, 81.

In the language of the translation widows may bequeath the crop, but Coke in his exposition of this chapter says, 'Before the making of this statute, it was a question, whether tenant in dower might *devise* the corn which she had sown, or whether he in reversion should have them. Some held that she could *devise* them; or if she devised them not, that her executors should not have them, etc.;' and he also says, in reference to the word legare in this chapter, which is represented in the translation by the word 'bequeath,' 'This word (legare) is appropriated to a last will, and signifieth to *bequeath* goods, chattels, and in some cases lands and tenements. Legatum a lege dicitur quia lege tenetur ille, cui interest perimplere.' So Shakespeare sometimes applies the word bequeath to Real Property.

Robert. Upon his death-bed he by will *bequeath'd*
His lands to me, and took it on his death
That this my mother's son was none of his ;
And if he were, he came into the world
Full fourteen weeks before the course of time.
Then, good my liege, let me have what is mine,
My father's land, as was my father's will.

.   .   .   .

Elinor. I like thee well : wilt thou forsake thy fortune,
Bequeath thy land to him and follow me ?
King John, Act i. Sc. 1.

VII.

To whom the elder did this aunswere frame ;
'Then weet ye, sir, that we two brethren be,
To whom our sire, Milesio by name,
Did equally *bequeath his lands in fee*,
Two islands, which ye there before you see
Not farre in sea ; of which the one appeares
But like a little mount of small degree ;
Yet was as great and wide ere many yeares,
As that same other isle, that greater bredth now beares.'
SPENSER, *Faerie Queene*, Book v. Canto 4.

Sometimes to personal property, as it is applied at the present day :

Orl. As I remember, Adam, it was upon this fashion *bequeathed* me by will but poor *a thousand crowns*, and, as thou sayest, charged my brother, on his blessing, to breed me well : and there begins my sadness.

As You Like It, Act i. Sc. 1.

Per. An *armour*, friends ! I pray you, let me see it.
Thanks, fortune, yet, that, after all my crosses,
Thou givest me somewhat to repair myself;
And though it was mine own, part of my heritage,
Which my dead father did *bequeath* to me.

Pericles, Act i. Sc. 1.

Ant. But here's a parchment with the seal of Cæsar;
I found it in his closet, 'tis his *will* :
Let but the commons hear this *testament*—
Which, pardon me, I do not mean to read—
And they would go and kiss dead Cæsar's wounds
And dip their napkins in his sacred blood,
Yea, beg a *hair* of him for memory,
And, dying, mention it within their wills,
Bequeathing it as a rich legacy
Unto their issue.

Julius Cæsar, Act iii. Sc. 2.

and sometimes he applies it to words and to things which do not suggest the idea of real or personal property :—

Jaq. You to your former *honour* I *bequeath*.

As You Like It, Act v. Sc. 4.

Yet die I will not till my Collatine
Have heard the cause of my untimely death;
That he may vow, in that sad hour of mine,
Revenge on him that made me stop my breath.
My *stained blood* to Tarquin I'll *bequeath*,
   Which by him tainted shall for him be spent,
   And as his due writ in my testament.

My *honour* I'll *bequeath* unto the knife
That wounds my body so dishonoured.
'Tis honour to deprive dishonour'd life;
The one will live, the other being dead:
So of shame's ashes shall my fame be bred!
   For in my death I murder shameful scorn:
   My shame so dead, mine honour is new-born.
                            Lucrece.

Cæs.   There is my hand.
A *sister* I *bequeath* you, whom no brother
Did ever love so dearly: let her live
To join our kingdoms and our hearts; and never
Fly off our loves again!
          Antony and Cleopatra, Act ii. Sc. 2.

Pan.   Brethren and sisters of the hold-door trade,
Some two months hence my will shall here be made:
It should be now, but that my fear is this,
Some galled goose of Winchester would hiss:
Till then I'll sweat and seek about for eases,
And at that time *bequeath you my diseases.*
          Troilus and Cressida, Act v. Sc. 10.

Lys.   You are unkind, Demetrius; be not so;
For you love Hermia; this you know I know:
And here, with all good will, with all my heart,
In Hermia's love I yield you up my part;

And yours of Helena to me *bequeath*,
Whom I do love and will do till my death.
> *A Midsummer Night's Dream*, Act iii. Sc. 2.

Paul.   'Tis time; descend; be stone no more; approach;
Strike all that look upon with marvel.   Come,
I'll fill your grave up: stir, nay, come away,
Bequeath to death your *numbness*, for from him
Dear life redeems you.
> *Winter's Tale*, Act v. Sc. 3.

P. Hen.   At Worcester must his body be interr'd;
For so he will'd it.
Bast.   Thither shall it then :
And happily may your sweet self put on
The lineal state and glory of the land !
To whom, with all submission, on my knee
I do *bequeath my faithful services*
And true subjection everlastingly.
> *King John*, Act v. Sc. 7.

X.

From thence it comes, that this babes bloody hand
May not be clensd with water of this well:
Ne certes, sir, strive you it to withstand,
But let them still be bloody, as befell,
That they his mothers innocence may tell,
As she *bequeathd* in her last testament;
That as a sacred symbole, it may dwell
In her sonnes flesh, to mind revengëment,
And be for all chaste dames an endlesse moniment.
> SPENSER, *Faerie Queene*, Book ii. Canto 2.

Laf.   I would it were not notorious.   Was this gentle-
woman the daughter of Gerard de Narbon ?
Count.   His sole child, my lord, and *bequeathed* to my
overlooking.
> *All's Well that Ends Well*, Act i. Sc. 1.

Thus it is evident that, in Shakespeare's time, the use of the word devise in a Will, in disposing of real property, or the omitting to use that word in disposing of the personal property, or even the use of the word bequeath in disposing of the personal property, or the omitting to use the word bequeath in disposing of the real property, would afford no evidence of technical skill, nor would the application of the word devise to personal property, or of the word bequeath to real property, afford evidence of a want of technical skill; because the few quotations I have made, from the old law writers, prove that before, during, and after Shakespeare's day, the words devise and bequeath were applied indifferently to both real and personal property.

Definitions are saide to be dangerous in lawe; the cause may be attributed to the multitude of different cases, the penurie of apt wordes, the weakness of our understanding and the contrarietie of opinions. For happely amongest such aboundant varietie of thinges, either we cannot discerne the true essence thereof, or we doo not aptly deliver what we conceave, or els these perils being past, at least in our owne opinions, yet are we still subject to the rigorous examination of all sorts of men, and must abide the doubtfull verdict of the sharpest wittes, and endure the dreadfull sentence of the deepest judgements. And it is rare if at the last, after long and superstitious revolution, *one man at least* among so many subtile heads and captious conceits doe not espie some defect or excesse in the definition, whereby the same may be subverted. Which thing if it come to pas, then like as when the captain is slaine, the souldiers are in danger to be discomfited; or as the foundation being *ruinous, the building is in peril of falling.*

Valentine. O thou that dost inhabit in my breast,
Leave not the mansion so long tenantless:
Lest, growing *ruinous, the building fall,*
And leave no memory of what it was!
Two Gentlemen of Verona, Act v. Sc. 4.

So the definition being overthrown, all the arguments drawn from thence and whatsoever els dependeth thereupon, is in perill to be overturned. No marvel then if definitions be reported to be dangerous.—*Swinburn*, 5.

Jaques de Bois. And to the skirts of this wild wood
he came;
Where meeting with an old religious man,
After some question with him, was converted
Both from his enterprise and from the world,
His *crown* bequeathing to his banish'd brother,
And all their lands restored to them again
That were with him exiled.
As You Like It, Act v. Sc. 4.

By the opinion of divers justices of this realme, and doctors of the cannon and civill lawe, the goodes of this realme, that is to say, of the auncient crowne, and jewelles, cannot be disposed by will.—*Swinburn*, 93.

But the word crown used by Jaques in this

passage may signify dominion or sovereignty,
or, as Schlegel says, ' Herrschaft':—

> Notwithstanding as well by the civill law as by the
> cannon lawe (with the which lawes the lawes of this our
> realme of England doe in this point seeme to joyne
> hands): It is unlawfull for a king to give awaie his
> kingdom from his lawfull heires, for the confirmation
> whereof divers writers use divers reasons.—*Swinburn*, 68.

> *Benedict.* Shall quips and sentences and these *paper
> bullets* of the brain awe a man from the career of his
> humour?
>
> *Much Ado About Nothing*, Act ii. Sc. 3.

> But amongst all their reasons, I see no reason to in-
> duce me to adventure anie further into the examination of
> this deepe and dangerous question, much lesse to pro-
> ceede to the conclusion; not onelie because the same
> being so high an object, dooth farre exceede the slender
> capacitie of a meane subjecte, but also for that this
> princlie controversie, as it hath seldome received ordi-
> narie triall heretofore; so hereafter, if the case were to
> be urged in verie deede, verie likelie it is to be urged
> with more violent arguments and sharpe syllogismes,
> then by the unbloodie blowes of bare words, or the
> weake *weapons of instruments made of paper and
> parchment*. And on the other side to bee answered
> with flatte denials of greater force, and distinctions of
> greater efficacie, then can proceede from anie legall or
> logicall engine, and in the end to be decided and ruled
> by the dead stroke of uncivill and martial cannons,
> rather than by anie rule of the civill or cannon lawe.—
> *Swinburn*, 68.

> *Bene.* I have almost matter enough in me for such
> an embassage; and so I *commit* you—

Claud.   To the *tuition* of God : From my house, if I had it.

> *Much Ado About Nothing*, Act i. Sc. 1.

Shakespeare, in this passage, uses testamentary language, and this meaning of the word tuition will appear from the following extracts :—

In the third part of this testamentarie treatise, there is to be shewed, firste what thinges, and then how much the testator maie dispose or devise by his testament.   Concerning the former of these, it shall not be a misse to speake first of the *bequeathing or devising of landes, tenements or hereditaments.*   Secondlie, of *bequeathing or devising of goods and cattelles* ; and thirdlie, of the *committing of the tuition* of children, and custodie of their portions and rights, during their minorities.—*Swinburn*, page 69.

By generall custome observed within the province of Yorke, the father by his last will or testament maie for a time *commit the* tuition of his childe, and the custodie of his portion, for within that province children have their filial portions of their father's goods according to the civill lawe, except he be heire or advanced in the life time of his father, which testament and assignation is to be confirmed by the ordinarie, who is also to provide for the execution of the same testament.   And if there be no tutor testamentarie at all, then maie the ordinarie commit the tuition of the childe to his next kinse-man. —*Swinburn*, 97.

In the old forms of wills, in assigning or appointing a tutor, the testator used words such as these: 'I commit my son to the tuition of A. B.;' and so much were the words 'commit' and 'tuition' used in connection with each other in making this appointment, that if the testator said 'I commit my son to A. B.,' omitting the word 'tuition,' it was presumed that he intended to use it, and that A. B. should be tutor to his child.

It *skilleth* not by what wordes the tutor be appointed, so that the testator's meaning doo appeare, for they are neverthelesse to bee confirmed tutors. Wherefore, if the testator saie I commit my children to the power of A. B. or leave them in his hands, it is in effect, as if the testator had said, I make A. B. tutor to my children; so it is if hee saie, I leave them to his governement, regiment, administration, &c. If the testator saie, I commit my sonne to A. B. both quicke and dead, with all his legacies by me given, by these wordes it is presumed that the testator meant that A. B. should be tutor to his child if he lived, and if he died, then to have those legacies. If the testator saie, I desire my wife to take care of my children during their minorities, albeit those wordes doo not necessarilie infer or conclude a tuition of their owne nature, but rather that she should chastice them, when they deserved to be corrected, (for to have tuition of children is a greater thinge and extendeth further then to have a care of them onelie:) Neverthelesse, for as much as the ruder sorte of people doe not know the difference of termes, nor the naturall force of wordes: Therefore, if any be assigned tutor by these foresaid words, he is to be confirmed. The same may be saide where the testator dooth commit his childe to the custodie of another. For, albeit it be a greater thinge to have the tuition of a childe, then to have the bare custodie of a child committed unto him: yet, in all thinges, the will and meaninge of the testator is to be observed and preferred before the propertie of the wordes, whereof perhaps he is ignorant, which meaning is to be collected by that which went before or followeth after in the will, and by other circumstances which the discreete judge ought to enquire. Finallie, it *skilleth* not in what language the tutor be assigned, whether in English, Latine, Greeke, or anie other tongue.—*Swinburn*, 101.

> *York.* It skills not greatly who impugns our doom.
> 2 *Henry VI.*, Act iii. Sc. 2.

> *Tra.* But to her love concerneth us to add
> Her father's liking: which to bring to pass,
> As I before imparted to your worship,
> I am to get a man,—whate'er he be,
> It *skills not* much, we'll fit him to our turn,—
> And he shall be Vincentio of Pisa.
> *Taming the Shrew*, Act iii. Sc. 2.

> *Clo.* Truly, madam, he holds Belzebub at the stave's end as well as a man in his case may do: has here writ a letter to you; I should have given 't you to-day morning, but as a madman's epistles are no gospels, so it *skills not* much when they are delivered.
> *Twelfth Night*, Act v. Sc. 1.

'Skills not,' matters not.

Swinburn's treatise contains many uncom-

mon words, or common words having an uncommon sense, which are used by Shakespeare.

> *Chor.* Now old desire doth in his death-bed lie,
>   And young affection *gapes* to be his heir;
> That fair for which love groan'd for and would die,
>   With tender Juliet match'd, is now not fair.
>> *Romeo and Juliet*, Act ii.

In a written testament the testator hath this benefit:
he maie conceale and keepe secreete the tenor or con-
tentes of his will, from the witnesses. Which he cannot
doe when he maketh a nuncupative testament. And
therefore if the testator be loath to have his will knowne,
which thing happeneth very often, either because the
testator is afraid to offende such persones as doo *gape*
for greater bequestes then either they have deserved, or
the testator is willing to bestowe upon them: (least they
peradventure understanding thereof, would not suffer
him to live in quiet), or else because hee should over
much encourage others, to whom he meante to bee more
beneficiall then they expected (and so give them occasion to be more negligent husbandes, or stewards, about
their owne affaires, then otherwise they would have beene,
if they had not expected such a benefit at the testator's
hands) or for some other considerations. In these and
like cases, after the testator hath written his will with
his owne hand, or procured some other to write the
same, he may close up the writing without making the
witnesses privie to the contents thereof, and shewing
the same to the witnesses, he may say unto them: This
is my last will and testament, or herein is contained my
wil: and this is sufficient.—*Swinburn*, 23.

Swinburn, speaking afterwards of testaments made by flatterie, says:—

The fifth case is, when the perswader is verie importunate : for an importunate begger is compared to an extortor, and it is an impudent part still to *gape* and crie upon the testator, and not to bee content with the first or second deniall.—243.

> *Leonato.* No, no; 'tis all men's office to speak patience
> To those that wring under the load of sorrow,
> But no man's virtue nor sufficiency
> To be so moral when he shall endure
> The like himself. Therefore give me no counsel :
> My griefs cry louder than *advertisement.*
>   *Much Ado About Nothing,* Act v. Sc. 1.

The word advertisement here signifies admonition, advice, exhortation, and in this sense it is often used by Swinburn.

Here followeth the fourthe principall part of this testamentary treatise : wherein I undertook to shew how or in what manner testaments or laste willes maie or ought to be made. For performance whereof I thought it convenient, first to deliver certaine *advertisements,* and then to proceede. The first *advertisement* is this, that as there be divers kindes of testaments or laste willes (whereof heretofore) so there be divers formes of testaments or laste willes : for everie kinde hath his severall forme, and everie kinde differeth from another by his forme. The next *advertisement* is this, that albeit everie particular kinde of testament have his proper forme peculier to it selfe; neverthelesse they have also generall formes common to them all.—*Swinburn,* 111.

Verg.   Yes, I thank God I am as honest as any man living that is an old man and no honester than I.

Dog.   *Comparisons are odorous*: palabras, neighbour Verges.

Much Ado About Nothing, Act iii. Sc. 5.

Comparisons be odious.   For mine own part, if you will give me leave, I will tell you a tale out of Zasius, writing upon this Q., which shall be as true as any is in Æsop's fables. A certaine painter (saith hee) meaning by his arte to describe the strength of man, did paint a little man riding upon a huge lion, as if a man were stronger than a lion. A lion passing by demanded of the painter, whereof he made such picture. Because (quoth the painter) my man is able to tame any lion, as easily as a horse or an asse. Well, sir, said the lion, if we could painte thou shouldst see a lion devouring a painter. Eloquent men are as painters, valiant souldiers as lions.—*Swinburn,* 28.

Clo.   Misprision in the highest degree! Lady, cucullus non facit monachum; that's as much to say as I wear not motley in my brain. Good madonna, give me leave to prove you a fool.

Twelfth Night, Act i. Sc. 5.

Escalus.   Signior Lucio, did not you say you knew that Friar Lodowick to be a dishonest person?

Lucio.   'Cucullus non facit monachum:' honest in nothing but in his clothes; and one that hath spoke most villanous speeches of the duke.

Measure for Measure, Act v. Sc. 1.

Hitherto in jest: But nowe in earnest, yet without offence. It is not the golden chaine, nor the plume of feathers, nor the bigge lookes, nor the proud bragges, which make a right souldier. Neither is it the long gown nor the grave beard, nor the stately gesture which make a good lawyer. The counterfeit of either deserveth no honour : be hee never so brave, never so grave. If both be as they should, the praeminence in matters of warre is the souldier's ; in matters of peace it is the lawyer's. In other matters, he is the more honourable, which doeth more honour the other.—*Swinburn*, page 29.

After the word lawyer in this passage, there is a reference to a marginal note giving the Latin words, twice used by Shakespeare, ' Cucullus non facit monachum.' (Swinburn, 28.)

Macb.   If you shall *cleave* to my consent, when 'tis,
It shall make honour for you.
> *Macbeth*, Act ii. Sc. 1.

Pros.   Come with a thought.   I thank thee, Ariel :
come.
> *Enter* ARIEL.

Ari.   Thy thoughts I *cleave to.* What's thy pleasure ?
> *Tempest*, Act iv. Sc. i.

Aum.   For ever may my knees grow to the earth,
My tongue *cleave* to my roof within my mouth,
Unless a pardon ere I rise or speak.
> *Richard II.*, Act v. Sc. 3.

Ban.   New honours come upon him,
Like our strange garments, *cleave* not to their mould
But with the aid of use.
> *Macbeth*, Act i. Sc. 3.

Clif. Plantagenet! I come, Plantagenet!
And this thy son's blood *cleaving* to my blade
Shall rust upon my weapon, till thy blood,
Congeal'd with this, do make me wipe off both.

3 Henry VI., Act i. Sc. 3.

Concerning the other two (the lawyer I meane and
the souldier) *whether* of them deserveth better of the
commonwealth, and *whether* is tŏ bee preferred before
the other, is a question so incident to this controversie,
and *cleaveth* so close thereunto, that there bee few writers
which handle the one, but they also touch the other.
In the determination whereof, if the interpreters of the
lawe may be judges in their owne cause, then the sentence must needes be, *cedant arma togae.*—*Swinburn,* 28.

'Whether,' often used by old authors for
'which.' 'Cleave,' to cling to, adhere.

   Isab.   I went
To this pernicious caitiff deputy,—
   Duke. That's somewhat madly spoken.
   Isab.   Pardon it;
The phrase is to the matter.
   Duke. Mended again. The matter; proceed.
   Isab. In brief, to set the needless process by,
How I persuaded, how I pray'd, and kneel'd,
How he *refell'd* me, and how I replied,—
For this was of much length,—the vile conclusion
I now begin with grief and shame to utter.

Measure for Measure, Act v. Sc. 1.

Albeit the childe be borne blind, or lame, yet is the
husbande presumed to have begotten the same, and not
the adulterer. In which case, neverthelesse some have

c 3

beene of this opinion, that this childe was begotten in
adulterie, being so borne (as they imagined) by God's
providence and justice, because of the sinne of the
parentes : whose rash opinion is by others *refelled* as
erronious and blinde.

I think I remember reading in this passage
in some edition of Shakespeare's Works the
word repelled for refelled. Swinburn uses
repelled often, but I remember seeing refelled
once only in his Treatise.

Mer. O, thou art deceived; I would have made it
short: for I was come to the whole depth of my tale;
and meant, indeed, to *occupy* the argument no longer.
Romeo and Juliet, Act ii. Sc. 4.

First Gent. A notable passion of wonder appeared in
them ; but the wisest beholder, that knew no more but
seeing, could not say if the *importance* were joy or sorrow ; but in the extremity of the one, it must needs be.
Winter's Tale, Act v. Sc. 1.

The limitations of this former conclusion are these :
First, when the testator doth in his testament give
licence to the legatarie to take and *occupie* the same,
without deliverie of the executor ; which licence may be
granted either expressly or secretly : expressly, when the
testator saith, I bequeath my horse to A. B., giving him
licence to take him, and to possesse, him of his owne authoritie, without any deliverie to be made by my executor: Secretly, when the testator saith, I bequeath unto
him my horse, which I will that he quietly enjoy without trouble or molestation; or by words of like *importance.—Swinburn,* 289.

Occupy, use.   Importance, here used by Shakespeare and Swinburn for import.

Cor.   Think upon me! hang 'em!
I would they would forget me, like the virtues
Which our divines lose by 'em.
Men.   You'll mar all:
I'll leave you: pray you, speak to 'em, I pray you,
In *wholesome manner.*

Coriolanus, Act ii. Sc. 3.

A Testament is defined to be a just sentence, we are to consider that this word just, hath divers significations in law. Sometimes it is opposed to that which is wicked or repugnant to justice, equitie, and to good and *wholesome manners.* Being taken in this sense, it giveth us to understand, that the testator cannot commande any thing that is wicked, or against justice, pietie, equity, honestie, &c. For things unlawfull are also reputed impossible: and therefore if the testator should commande any such thing in his testament, the same were not to be observed. As if he should wil any man to be murthered; for this is against the law of God: or if he should commande his body to be cast into the river, for this is against humanitie; or if he should commande his goods to be burned, for this is against policie; or if he should commande any ridiculous acte, or prejudiciall onely to his owne credite and dignitie; as if he should will his buriall or *funerals* to be solemnised with May-games or Morrice daunces, for this were to manifest his follie, or at least to make question whether he were of sound minde and memorie. In these and the like cases the Executor in not performing the commandements or requests of the testator is not onely holden excused, but is highly commended.—*Swinburn*, page 6.

> *Marc.*   Suffer thy brother Marcus to inter
> His noble nephew here in virtue's nest,
> That died in honour and Lavinia's cause.
> Thou art a Roman; be not barbarous:
> The Greeks upon advice did bury Ajax
> That slew himself; and wise Laertes' son
> Did graciously plead for his *funerals*:
>> *Titus Andronicus*, Act i. Sc. 2.

Funerals.   This word is used several times by Swinburn.

> *Gloucester.*   *Naughty* lady.
>> *Lear*, Act iii. Sc. 7.

> *Bolingbroke.*   My rights and royalties,
> Pluck'd from my arms perforce, and given away
> To upstart *unthrifts*.
>> *Richard II.*, Act ii. Sc. 3.

> *Macbeth.*   Methought I heard a voice cry 'Sleep no
>   more!
> Macbeth does murder sleep,' the innocent sleep,
> Sleep that knits up the ravell'd sleave of care,
> The death of each day's life, *sore labour's* bath,
> Balm of hurt minds, great nature's second course,
> Chief nourisher in life's feast.
>> *Macbeth*, Act ii. Sc. 2.

> *Timon.*   Although, I know, you'll swear, terribly
>   swear
> Into strong shudders and to heavenly agues
> The immortal gods that hear you,—spare your oaths,
> I'll trust to your *conditions*: be whores still.
>> *Timon of Athens*, Act iv. Sc. 3.

In the opinion of some, the lawe of this land which
leaveth all the residue to the disposition of the testator,
funeralles and debts deducted, seemeth to have better
grounde in reason, then the custome, whereby he is
forced either to leave two partes of three, or at least the
one halfe to his wife and children. For what if the
sonne be an *unthrifte* or *naughtie* person, what if the
wife be not onlie a sharpe *shrowe*, but perhaps of worse
conditions? Is it not harde that the testator must leave
either the one halfe of his goods to that wife or child or
more, for the which also peradventure hee had *labored
full· sore* all his life? were it not more reason that it
should be in the libertie of the father, or husband to
dispose thereof at his owne pleasure? which when the
wife and children understood, it might be a means
whereby they might become more obedient, live more
vertuoslie, and contend with good desert, to winne the
good will and favour of the testator. These reasons make
for the testator, and for the equitie of the common law,
which leaveth the whole residue to his disposition. But
the custome whereby the libertie of the testator is re-
strained is not without reason also. For where it is
asked, what if the child be an *unthrifte*, the wife worse
then a *shrowe?* So it maie be demanded with like faciltie,
what if the wife be no *unthrifte*, but frugall and ver-
tuous? what if the wife be an *honest* and modest woman?
which thing is the rather to be presumed. But if it be
not amisse to feare the worst, then on the contrarie,
what if the testator be an unnaturall father or unkinde
husband? perhaps also greatly enriched by his wife,
whereas before he was but poore, standeth it not with
as great reason that such a wife and children should be
provided for, and that it shoulde not be in the power of
such a testator, to give all from them, or to bestowe it

upon such as had not so well deserved it, and by that
meanes set his wife and children a begging? Surelie the
custome hath as good ground in reason against lewd
husbands and unkinde fathers, as hath the lawe in meeting with disobedient wives and *unthrifty* children.—
Swinburn, p. 106.

Several words are used in this passage, as
they are sometimes by Shakespeare, in senses
different from those which they now convey;
as naughty for bad, wicked; full for very;
honest for virtuous or chaste; condition for
temper, quality, inclination; and Swinburn
here speaks of one who 'had *labored* full *sore*
all his *life*,' and Shakespeare of,

The death of each day's *life, sore labour's* bath.

Shakespeare often uses these words in these
senses, although I give only a few examples.

Olivia.   Were you sent here to praise me?
Twelfth Night, Act i. Sc. 5.

The verb to praise signifying to appraise, or
value, is used in some of our old law books
and ancient statutes (Swinburn, Henry VIII.
21, c. 5, and others), which speak of the form
to be observed in making an inventory; and
Olivia speaking of an inventory (see p. 9) uses

it in that sense, so also does Launce who plays upon the word:

Launce. She hath more qualities than a water-spaniel; which is much in a bare Christian. [*Pulling out a paper.*] Here is the cate-log of her *conditions.* . 'Imprimis: she can fetch and carry.' Why, a horse can do no more: nay, a horse cannot fetch, but only carry; therefore is she better than a jade. 'Item: she can milk;' look you, a sweet virtue in a maid with clean hands.

. . . .

Speed. 'Item: She will often praise her liquor.'
Launce. If her liquor be good, she shall: if she will not, I will; for *good things* should be *praised.*

Two Gentlemen of Verona, Act iii. Sc. 1.

Launce (whose Cate-log resembles Olivia's inventory) says *good* things should be *praised,* and an inventory contained a description of the *goods* with their value *appraised;* or to use Swinburn's words, ' The *things* that are to be put into the inventorie, are all the *goods,* and cattels, and rights, which were the testator's.' 218.

It is not sufficient to make an inventorie, containing all and singular the *goods* of the deceased, unless the same be particularly *valued* and *praised* by some honest and skilfull persons, to be the just value thereof in their judgements and consciences, that is to say, at such price as the same may be solde for at that time. In ancient time, amongst many other solemnities of inventories, this order was observed: First of all, the moveable *goods* were inventoried and *praised*, as household stuffe, corne, and cattell, &c. ; then the immoveable, as leases of groundes or tenements, after that the debts due to the testator were set downe, which order is for the most parte observed at this time here in England: saving that some doo omit leases, wherein they do amisse: others *praise* them among the moveables, but it were better to *praise* them severally.—*Swinburn*, 220.

Richmond.   Abate the edge of traitors, gracious Lord,
That would *reduce* these bloody days again,
And make poor England weep in streams of blood.
                              Richard III., Act v. Sc. 5.

Burgundy.   And as our vineyards, fallows, meads, and
                        hedges,
Defective in their natures, grow to wildness,
Even so our houses and ourselves and children
Have lost, or do not learn for want of time,
The sciences that should become our country ;
But grow like savages,—as soldiers will
That nothing do but meditate on blood,—
To swearing and stern looks, diffused attire
And everything that seems unnatural.
Which to *reduce* into our former favour
You are assembled :
                              Henry V., Act v. Sc. 2.

Reduce, bring back, used in this sense by Swinburn,

When the testator and legatarie be reconciled and *reduced* into friendship againe, then the former enimities do not prejudice the legatarie.—*Swinburn*, page 288.

When the thing bequeathed, whereof the former is altered, may be *reduced* to his first matter ; as when the testator doth bequeath some masse of metall be it gold or silver, tinne, or such like, whereof the testator afterwardes dooth make some vessell, or other instrument. Or on the contrarie, the testator having bequeathed a cuppe of golde, or other vessell, or instrument of metall, dooth afterwardes *dissolve* the same to his first matter : or the testator having bequeathed a cup of golde dooth make a chaine thereof : the will of the testator by such alterations is not presumed to be altered, and therefore the legacie is not thereby extinguished. But if the thing bequeathed after the forme thereof be altered, cannot be *reduced* to that which it was before; as wool when it is made clothe : or timber when it is hewen or made parcell of a ship : the testator having bequeathed certaine wool or timber, and afterwards translating the same to other forms, from whence they cannot be *reduced* to the former, the legacie is extinguished, unlesse it doo appeare that the will of the testator therein is not chaunged.—*Swinburn,* 294.

Othello. Now, how dost thou look, O ill-starr'd *wench !* Pale as thy smock. Act v. Sc. 2.

By the said custome generallie observed within the province of Yorke, a Tutor maie be assigned to a boie at anie time untill hee have accomplished the age of 14 yeeres, and to a *wench* until she have accomplished the age of twelve yeeres.—*Swinburn,* 98.

The word wench is frequently used by Shakespeare in a good sense, as it is by Queen Katherine in Henry V^{III}. and by Swinburn in this passage.

Laertes.   Think it no more :
For nature, crescent, does not grow alone
In thews and bulk, but, as this temple waxes,
The inward service of the mind and soul
Grows wide withal.   Perhaps he loves you now,
And now no soil nor *cautel doth besmirch*
The virtue of his will : but you must fear,
His greatness weigh'd, his *will* is not his own ;
For he himself is subject to his birth :
He may not, as unvalued persons do,
Carve for himself; for on his choice depends
The safety and health of this whole state ;
And therefore must his choice be circumscribed
Unto the voice and yielding of that body
Whereof he is the head.

Hamlet, Act i. Sc. 3.

Shakespeare may have written these verses remembering the following passages from Swinburn's Treatise on Wills.

It is an old question, whether he that hath taken an oth not to make a testament, may notwithstanding make a testament: and although there were many which did hold that in this case he could not make a testament, yet the greater number are of the contrarie opinion ; esteeming the othe not to be lawfull, and consequently not of force to deprive a man of the libertie of making a testament.   And therefore if a man first make a testament, and then sweareth never to revoke the same, yet notwithstanding he may make another testament and thereby revoke the former : for *there is no cautele under heaven, whereby the libertie of making or revoking his testament can be utterly taken away.*—*Swinburn*, 61.

The clause derogatorie of the power of making testaments is utterly voide in law, neither can a man renounce
be power or libertie of making testaments, neither is
here any *cautele* under heaven to prevent this libertie;
which also indureth whiles any life indureth, as hath
bene aforesaid.—*Swinburn*, 266.

So large and ample is the libertie of making testaments,
that a man may as oft as hee will make a newe testament,
even untill the last breath, neither is there any *cautele*
under the sunne to prevent this libertie.—*Swinburn*, 263.

In the alphabetical table of the particular
contents of this treatise of Swinburn's are
these words, 'No *cautell* can take away the
libertie of making a testament.'

Laertes says, 'no soil nor cautel doth besmirch the virtue of his will,' and Swinburn
'there is no cautele under heaven, whereby
the libertie of making or revoking his testament can be utterly taken away.' Again
Laertes says,

> *He may not*, as unvalued persons do
> *Carve for himself.*

And according to Swinburn, 'it is not lawful
for legataries to *carve for themselves*, taking
their legacies at their own pleasure, but must
have them delivered by the executors.' (Swinburn, 50.)

If the legatarie of his owne authoritie without th
consent of the executor, do apprehend and *occupie* th
legacie to him bequeathed, he loseth his right and in
terest thereunto : *For he may not be his own carver* ii
this case, but ought to receive his legacie at the hande
of the executor : which executor ought first to have al
the goods and cattels in his hands, for the paiment and
discharge of the testator's debts, which debts ought tc
be paid before legacies.—*Swinburn*, 289.

APPENDIX A.

Dogberry. Marry, sir, they have committed false report; moreover, they have spoken untruths; secondarily, they are slanders; sixth and lastly, they have belied a lady; thirdly, they have verified unjust things; and, to conclude, they are lying knaves.—*Much Ado About Nothing*, Act v. Sc. 1.

SHAKESPEARE A LAWYER' was published the first week in August 1858. It was an attempt to illustrate some obscure passages, and to show that Shakespeare had acquired a general knowledge of the principles and practice of the Law of Real Property, of the Common Law and Criminal Law, that he was familiar with the exact letter of the Statute Law, and that he used law terms *correctly*; and Lord Campbell says, page 107 :—' Having concluded my examination of Shakespeare's judicial phrases and forensic allusions,—on the retrospect I am amazed, not only by their number, but by the *accuracy and propriety* with which they are uniformly introduced. There is nothing so dangerous as for one not of the craft to tamper with our free masonry.'

Long after 'Shakespeare a Lawyer' had bee
much and favourably reviewed, and was well know
in England, Scotland, and Germany, the followin
paragraph appeared in a literary paper in London :-

A new illustrator of Shakspeare has entered the field in th
person of the Lord Chief Justice of the Queen's Bench, Lor
Campbell. During a recent vacation in Scotland, he turne
his attention again to our great dramatic poet, and reading ove
his plays consecutively, he was struck by the vast number o
legal phrases and allusions they contain, and by the extrem
appropriateness and accuracy of their application. He beg
noting them, giving them such explanations and elucidatio
as his vast experience and knowledge of the law enabled hi
readily to furnish. He has since put them into more regul
form and order, and is printing them in the shape of a famili
letter to Mr. Payne Collier.

Soon after this announcement was made, Lor
Campbell's book was published, and reviewed i
several of the London papers, some of them contrast
ing it with my pamphlet, as the following extract
will show :—

Were we to put faith in circumstantial evidence and give n
weight to evidence of character, we probably should find Lor
Campbell guilty upon the charge of having robbed a mare'
nest. Robbery of a mare's nest by the Lord Chief Justice is
however, an impossible offence. We are content then simply
to remark upon the accidental fact that for all pertinent cita-
tions produced by the Chief Justice from Shakespeare's play
in confirmation of Malone's theory that the poet picked up law
in an attorney's office, his lordship, when he wrote his letter to
Mr. Collier, might have referred to the then extant pamphlet
of a Liverpool attorney.* Mr. Rushton's little publication was
already in print when, on the fifteenth of last September, Lord
Campbell dated the first lines of the argument which he now

* Then a student-at-law.

publishes. In 'Household Words' about three months ago, attention was directed to the argument of Mr. Rushton in an article that, under the head of ' Mr. W. Shakespeare, Solicitor,' treated it with friendly ridicule. Unluckily, the existence of the previous publication, which contains all his discoveries, did not become known to Lord Campbell.—*The Examiner*, London, January 29, 1859.

The greatest error that can be laid to his lordship's charge is, that he completely ignores the existence of a little book which runs *pari passu* with his own inquiry. It is scarcely three months since a Mr. W. L. Rushton, of Liverpool, published a very modest pamphlet, entitled 'Shakespeare a Lawyer,' and in this unpretending work may be found all, and more than all, the quotations in Lord Campbell's work, with a full and able comment upon the arguments to be derived from them. In illustration, we need only point out the way Mr. Rushton commentates on the passage relating to *præmunire*, in which he dilates on the peculiarly legal mode in which Shakespeare uses his legal phraseology. He claims for the poet a knowledge not only of the principles and practice of the law of real property, but also of the common law, and a thorough intimacy with the exact letter of the statute law.—*The Critic*, London, February 5, 1859.

After these reviews appeared, the London *Times* contained a long and laudatory notice of Lord Campbell's work, which did not mention my pamphlet or my name. Then two works on Shakespeare's various knowledge were brought out, which praised highly Lord Campbell and his book, but said nothing of me or my pamphlet. In some of the biographical notices of Shakespeare, published in England and Scotland at the time of the Tercentenary, and in many of the addresses delivered on that occasion, Lord Campbell and his work were mentioned, but none of them spoke of W. L. Rushton, or ' Shakes-

peare a Lawyer.' I have been informed that
several of the New York papers in the year 1858
or 1859 reviewed very kindly 'Shakespeare a
Lawyer,' but in the year 1867 a work on Shakespeare was published in that city which speaks much
of Lord Campbell and his book, but says nothing
of me or mine. 'Sixth and lastly': The Cata-
logue of Books does not mention 'Shakespeare a
Lawyer,' but 'Shakespeare's Legal Maxims,' of
which a second edition has not yet been published,
is therein thus described:—

Rush (*sic*) W. L. Shakespeare's Legal Maxims, second ed.
flscp. Longmans, 1*s*.

This is a brief statement of the facts of the case.

I would to God my name were not so terrible to the enemy
as it is.

Falstaff, 2 *Henry IV.* Act. i. Sc. 2.

APPENDIX B.

These are Lord Campbell's words:—

In his will, when originally engrossed, there was no notice whatever taken of his wife; but immediately after these limitations, he subsequently interpolated a bequest to her in the following words:—'I give unto my wife my second best bed, with the furniture.'

The subject of this magnificent gift being only personal property, he shews his technical skill by omitting the word *devise*, which he had used in disposing of his realty.—Page 106.

'While novelists and dramatists' (says Lord Campbell, page 108) 'are constantly making mistakes as to the law of marriage, of wills, and of inheritance, to Shakespeare's law, lavishly as he propounds it, there can be neither demurrer, nor bill of exceptions, nor writ of error.

This cannot be said of Lord Campbell's law as he propounds it in his ' Shakespeare's Legal Acquirements Considered.' Novelists and dramatists are not the only writers who are constantly making mistakes as to the law of marriage, of wills, and inheritance.

King. Then for the place where; where, I mean, I did encounter that obscene and most preposterous event, that draweth from my snow-white pen the ebon-coloured ink, which here thou viewest, beholdest, surveyest, or seest:

.   .   .   .

Him I, as my ever-esteemed duty pricks me on, have sent to thee, to receive the meed of punishment, by thy sweet grace's officer, Anthony Dull; a man of good repute, carriage, bearing, and estimation.

Love's Labour Lost, Act i. Sc. 1.

Of this passage Lord Campbell says:—

It is drawn up in the true lawyer-like, tautological dialect,—which is to be paid for at so much a folio. The gifted Shakespeare might perhaps have been capable, by intuition, of thus imitating the conveyancer's jargon; but no ordinary man could have hit it off so exactly, without having engrossed in an attorney's office.—Page 47.

I have shown ('Shakespeare Illustrated by Old Authors,'* 2nd Part, page 14), that Shakespeare in this and many other passages uses the figure of Store, for he here speaks of that 'obscene and most preposterous *event*,' multiplying speech by using many words of one sense, 'viewest, beholdest, surveyest, or seest,' and Puttenham, speaking of the figure of Store, says, 'The Latines having no fitte terms to give him called it by a name of *event*.' Shakespeare also probably uses this figure in *Hamlet*, Act v. Sc. 1., where the first Clown multiplies his speech by using words of one sense thus,—'An act hath three branches: it is to do, to act, to perform,' although it was in the last century suggested that Shakespeare here refers to a case in Plowden's Reports 'Hales v. Petit':—

Let a non-professional man, however acute (says Lord Campbell, page 109), presume to talk law, or to draw illustrations from legal science in discussing other subjects, and he will speedily fall into some laughable absurdity.

* See Appendix C.

If Lord Campbell had ever engrossed in an attorney's office or known more of what he calls the conveyancer's jargon, he would not, probably, have fallen into a laughable absurdity in describing the words in *Troilus and Cressida*, Act iii. Sc. 2, ' In witness whereof the parties interchangeably,'—as the exact form of the *testatum* clause of an indenture.

These are Lord Campbell's words:—

The advice of Pandarus to the lovers being taken, he exclaims—
' What! billing again? Here's In witness the parties interchangeably.' The exact form of the *testatum* clause in an indenture. ' In witness whereof the parties interchangeably have hereto set their hands and seals.' Page 78.

Mark now how a plain tale shall put you down.
1 *Henry IV.*, Act. ii. Sc. 4.

Lord Campbell says, page 49 :—

In Act i. Sc. 3, and Act ii. Sc. 8, Antonio's bond to Shylock is prepared and talked about according to all the forms observed in an English attorney's office. The distinction between ' a single bill and a bond with a condition ' is clearly referred to.

The distinction between a single bond and a bond with a condition is not clearly referred to in the *Merchant of Venice*, although the following passage from ' Shakespeare a Lawyer,' which explains the difference between a single bond and a bond with a condition may have created that impression :—

An obligation, according to our common law, is a bond containing a penalty, with a condition for payment of money ; or to do or suffer some act or thing, &c. If it is without condition, it is called a *bill*, which is sometimes with a penalty, and then it is called a penal *bill*, or simple bond. An obligation or *bond* is a deed whereby the obligor obliges himself, his heirs, executors, or administrators, to pay a certain sum of money to another at a day appointed. If this be all, the bond is a single one, *simplex obligatio.*

> *Shylock.* Go with me to a notary, seal me there
> Your *single bond.*

But a condition is generally added, that if the obligor does some particular act, the obligation shall be void, as performance of covenants, or repayments of a principal sum borrowed of the obligee, with interest, which sum is usually one-half of the penal sum named in the bond.

> Say for non-payment that the debt should *double.*
> > *Venus and Adonis.*

> *Portia.* What sum owes he the Jew ?
> *Bassanio.* For me, three thousand ducats.
> *Portia.*   What, no more ?
> Pay him six thousand and deface the bond.
> > *Merchant of Venice,* Act iii. Sc. 4.

Bonds, with conditions of this kind annexed, have been long in use, and in former times on a conditional bond becoming forfeited for non-payment of the money borrowed, the *whole* penalty, usually double the principal sum lent by the obligee, was recoverable. So Macbeth says :—

> But yet I'll make assurance *double* sure,
> And take a bond of fate.
> > Act. iv. Sc. 1.

Referring not to a single, but to a conditional bond, under, or by virtue of which, when forfeited, double the principal sum was recoverable.—*Shakespeare a Lawyer,* page 19.

In ' Shakespeare a Lawyer,' and *nowhere else,* it may appear that the distinction between a single bond and a bond with a condition annexed, ' is clearly referred ' to in the *Merchant of Venice,* for although in my pamphlet it seems that Shylock mentions only a single bond, yet, as the reader will see—

Shylock. Go with me to a notary, seal me there
Your single bond : and, in a merry sport,
If you repay me not on such a day,
In such a place, such sum or sums as are
Express'd in the *condition,* let the forfeit
Be nominated for an equal pound
Of your fair flesh, to be cut off and taken
In what part of your body pleaseth me.
Merchant of Venice, Act i. Sc. 3,

He afterwards, in the same passage, speaks of such sum or sums as are expressed in the *condition!*

Hear, Land o' Cakes, and brither Scots,
Frae Maidenkirk to Johnny Groat's ;—
If there's a hole in a' your coats,
I rede you tent it :
A chield's amang you taking notes,
And, faith, he'll prent it.

We all know that Lord Campbell was a lawyer of great experience, yet in his book he has made several mistakes in law ; how, then, could any errors in law which I might show in Shakespeare's works afford conclusive evidence that Shakespeare was not a lawyer ?

APPENDIX C.

THE GUARDIAN, *January* 23, 1867.

Mr. Rushton has before now written a book to prove that Shakespeare was a lawyer; but the first part of his present work—*Shakespeare Illustrated by Old Authors* (Longmans)—does not aim at proving anything in particular. Its object is to explain obscure passages and expressions of doubtful meaning which occur in Shakespeare by reference to other old writers—not necessarily to writers older then Shakespeare, for Selden, Coke, and Burton, the Burton of 'Melancholy' fame, are among Mr. Rushton's authorities. The explanations and illustrations thus given are sometimes valuable and almost always interesting. After full allowance for accidental coincidences, it is quite clear that Shakespeare welcomed knowledge from whatever quarter it came, and knew how to turn even its fragments to account. The passages quoted by Mr. Rushton contain satisfactory evidence that Shakespeare, when he began to write for the stage, was a student of Puttenham's ' Arte of English Poesie,' then quite a new book. This discursive and amusing little volume ends with an elaborate discussion of the true meaning of ' Esquire.'

THE GUARDIAN, *June* 10, 1868.

Mr. Lowes Rushton has now issued a second part of his *Shakespeare Illustrated by Old Authors* (Longmans). Like the former part, it contains much that will interest lovers of our earlier literature ;

some of the coincidences between Shakespeare and Spenser which Mr. Rushton has noted are exceedingly curious. The two parts bound together form a very pleasing little book.

THE MORNING STAR, *February* 10, 1868.

Shakespeare Illustrated by Old Authors (Longmans) is the title of a somewhat curious and very interesting little work, by Mr. William Lowes Rushton. The object of the author is to collect the most remarkable instances of similar thoughts expressed in somewhat similar words by Shakespeare, and by authors, English or foreign, who preceded or were contemporaneous with him. One practical and scholarly purpose in this collection is frequently to elucidate the meaning of some doubtful phrase in Shakespeare by showing how it was used by older English authors, or by his contemporaries. But another object is to endeavour to ascertain the nature and extent of Shakespeare's reading, by discovering where and when he has introduced certain reflections, or employed certain phrases which seem directly inspired by the pages of some preceding writer. Mr. Rushton does not suggest that Shakespeare plagiarised, or even imitated; but as every man's style is necessarily influenced by the memory of what he reads, the author of this little work thinks that such a collection as his may serve to teach us what Shakespeare's tastes and favourite writers were. Very curious indeed are some of the parallel passages Mr. Rushton cites. In some, however, the resemblance is but faint; a few, we think, are positively strained to help out a theory. But the amount of reading displayed in the work is quite uncommon, and the lavishness of quotation with which its objects are illustrated make it a very anthology of poetry and prose. Students of Shakespeare will find their curiosity piqued by this little book; and it is delightful reading for anyone who feels an interest in comparing the thoughts and phrases of great authors.

THE ATHENÆUM, *February* 29, 1868.

The object of the book is to throw light upon Shakespeare's meanings and allusions by reference to other writers, either contemporaneous with him or previous to him.   Amongst the former, Puttenham, in 'The Arte of English Poesie,' repeatedly figures.   But Mr. Rushton frequently ascends to classical authors for his parallels and expositions.   The sources drawn upon for illustration in the book are numerous and varied—ancient poets, chroniclers, antiquaries, legal sages, literary essayists, and forgotten gossips.   Sometimes the illustrations which they afford are vague and purely conjectural ; but in many cases they are pertinent and valuable.   Altogether, we may pronounce this a conscientious and able book, full of particulars which are often valuable in casting light upon Shakespeare, and which, with scarcely an exception, are interesting in themselves.

LONDON: PRINTED BY
SPOTTISWOODE AND CO., NEW-STREET SQUARE
AND PARLIAMENT STREET

www.ingramcontent.com/pod-product-compliance
Lightning Source LLC
Chambersburg PA
CBHW030719110426
42739CB00030B/996